Editor
Nicole Lagneau
Picture Research
Jenny Golden
Production
Eva Wrennall
Consultant
Michael Fish, BBC broadcaster,
Meteorological officer at the London
Weather Centre
Teacher Panel
Shimon Levison
Andrew McLeod
Roy Williams
Illustrators
Dinah Cohen
Kate Lloyds-Jones/Linden Artists Ltd
Denis Manton/Linda Rogers Associates
David Mostyn/Linda Rogers Associates

Published in the United
States by Silver Burdett
Company, Morristown, N.J.
1980 Printing

ISBN 0 382 06394 5

Library of Congress
Catalog Card No. 80-50958

Photographic credits
Tony Duffy/All Sport 31
(top); Gerald Clyde/
Barnaby's Picture Library
7 (top); Barnaby's Picture
Library 28; BBC 37 (top);
Church Missionary
Society 11; John Cleare 7
(bottom); Eric Crichton 9;
Robert Harding Associates
18/19; Library of
Congress 25; Mansell
Collection 42; Meteoro-
logical Office/Crown
Copyright 16; P. Morris
14, 28/29, 41 (left); Tony
Morrison 31 (bottom);
Museum of London 40;
NASA 17 (top); Oxfam
41 (right); R. K. Pilsbury
20/21 (bottom), 22, 23,
29, 37 (bottom);
Popperfoto 17 (bottom);
Shaun Skelley 35;
Spectrum Colour Library
24/25, 33, 38, 39; United
States Information
Service 43 (bottom);
Jerry Young 12;
V. Englebert/ZEFA 20/21
(top); W. Fritz/ZEFA 32;
Dr W. Loewe/ZEFA 27;
ZEFA 8, Cover.

Weather

Roy Woodcock

Macdonald Educational

Contents

How to use this book
This book tells you about weather. In it you will find out what weather is all about, why it rains in some places most of the time while other places are dry all the year round. For instance if you want to find out about depressions, you will see that depressions are on page 14. The index will tell you where and how many times a particular subject is listed and whether there is a picture of it. Clouds, for example, you will find on page 22. The glossary explains the more difficult terms found in this book.

What is weather?

Weather is part of our lives. It affects the way we dress, the food we eat, the type of house we live in. Weather forecasters try to find out why a place has been so wet or dry and whether it is going to be warm or cold. They record temperatures, wind speed, pressure and rainfall of a particular place in order to make a weather forecast. The study of weather is called meteorology.

The average weather of a place over a period of time is called climate. For instance, in India there is a regular pattern of warm and dry winters whereas summers are hot and wet.

A sea of air

.The Earth is surrounded by a 'sea' of air called the atmosphere. It is made up of layers of gases that protect us from extremes of heat or cold. The lowest layer of the atmosphere, the troposphere, contains water vapour and it is there that the weather is found.

Air has weight which presses upon everything. The pressure is greatest at sea level but decreases with height. Aeroplanes have to be capable of withstanding these pressure changes. Mountain climbers find it difficult to breathe when they climb high mountains because of the lack of oxygen in the air at high altitude.

People and weather

People in different parts of the world have different types of houses because of the variation in weather conditions. In Norway, houses often have steeply sloping roofs to allow the rain to rush away quickly. But in Switzerland, the roofs have gentle slopes which allow snow to stay there without falling off. This helps to insulate the house by keeping the warmth from escaping.

People dress according to the weather. In the Arctic it is always cold and local inhabitants wear warm clothes. Near the equator, it is hot during the day but cool at night so people wear light cloaks. In these two areas the weather is much the same every day and so the weather is the same as the climate.

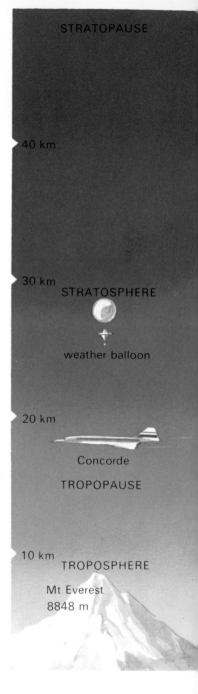

STRATOPAUSE

40 km

30 km
STRATOSPHERE

weather balloon

20 km

Concorde

TROPOPAUSE

10 km
TROPOSPHERE

Mt Everest
8848 m

▲ The atmosphere is very thin above the tropopause. Changes in the weather only affect the troposphere. Concorde flies higher than the weather.

▲ Strong winds make rough seas.

Mountain climbers wear oxygen masks to get the extra oxygen they need at high altitude. ▶

'The North wind doth blow and we shall have snow.'

Temperature

The heat that we have on the Earth all comes from the sun. The sun's rays all travel parallel to one another and they are at right angles to the equator. At mid-day, the sun at the equator is directly overhead and the sun's rays have the shortest possible journey through the atmosphere.

Heat from the sun is always the same, it is constant. The diagram below shows that because the Earth is curved, the sun's rays are spread over a greater area near the poles than near the equator. They also have to travel through a greater thickness of atmosphere at the poles.

The sun brings heat and energy towards the Earth. Some does not reach the ground but is reflected or absorbed by clouds or dust particles. ▶

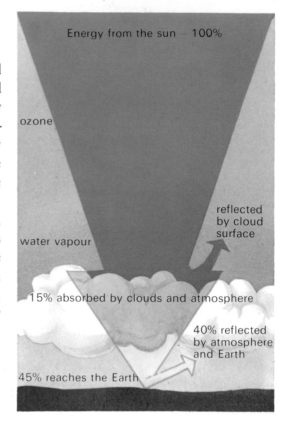

Energy from the sun – 100%

ozone

water vapour

reflected by cloud surface

15% absorbed by clouds and atmosphere

40% reflected by atmosphere and Earth

45% reaches the Earth

◀ The sun's rays are all parallel. They have a shorter journey through the atmosphere to the equator than to the poles. So temperatures decrease from the equator to the poles.

N. Pole

sun's rays

equator

S. Pole

atmosphere

In the Sahara desert Arabs wear light cloaks and turbans to protect them-selves from heat and sand. ▼

Therefore temperatures decrease from the equator to the poles.

The sun heats both land and sea, but land absorbs heat much more quickly than sea. The ocean currents also spread the heat around the oceans.

In summer the sea is cooler than the land for these reasons, but in winter, the land loses heat quickly whereas the sea will retain its warmth for a much longer time.

The oceans around Britain may still be as warm in November as they were in early summer. The oceans are like night storage heaters or hot water bottles which retain some warmth for a few hours after their source of heat has gone.

Some parts of the world have high temperatures and hot weather all the time, but others have hot seasons. In southern Australia or Canada, for example, the summer is much warmer than the winter whereas in central Africa it is hot the whole year round.

In some countries there are occasional hot spells which may last for a few weeks and these are called heatwaves. Most of the heatwaves which affect Britain occur when southerly winds bring very warm air from further south.

The hottest weather in the USA will also accompany southerly winds, but in the southern hemisphere the hottest weather will come with northerly winds. In Argentina or Australia, the dry and very hot weather associated with winds blowing from the north can be unpleasant, and may even make people's skin crack, because of the lack of moisture in the air.

Temperatures are very important in deciding where to go on holiday. In the USA for instance many people go to Florida in winter because it is much warmer than New York or Washington. In Britain and Northern Europe millions of tourists go to the Mediterranean countries because they are much sunnier in the summer.

The words hot and cold are not always very clear or accurate, and may mean different things to different people. For example a Malaysian may talk about his cold season, which is when the temperature falls to about 21°C, but to an Englishman this figure would mean warm weather.

The roof of greenhouses lets the sun's rays go through, but traps heat reflected back from the ground. This keeps greenhouses hot enough to grow plants and vegetables out of season. ▼

Atmospheric circulation

Hot air rises. The heat of the sun causes air to rise at or near the equator. This hot air circles around the upper atmosphere, cools and then drops. The main mass of falling air descends somewhere near the tropics though some travels as far as the Arctic and Antarctic before falling.

The air which falls at the tropics spreads out on reaching ground level, and travels north and south. It forms surface winds. These winds either blow back towards the equator and are called *trade winds*, or they blow away from the equator as *westerlies*.

Cold heavy air sinks. The falling air causes regions of air pressure which are the source of the major winds. The polar regions are cold and therefore have masses of falling air. They too are source regions for winds.

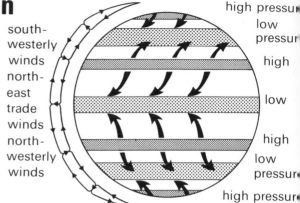

south-westerly winds
north-east trade winds
north-westerly winds

high pressure
low pressure
high
low
high
low pressure
high pressure

▲ The main winds blow from the tropical and polar high pressure regions, to the temperate and equatorial low pressure zones. The tropical winds are called trade winds and they blow towards the equator. The westerlies are temperate winds and blow from the tropical high pressure zones towards the poles.

The Equatorial current of the North Atlantic flows from east to west across the ocean because the winds blow water in that direction. The current turns to its right because of the effect of the rotation of the Earth, and the shape of the coastline. ▼

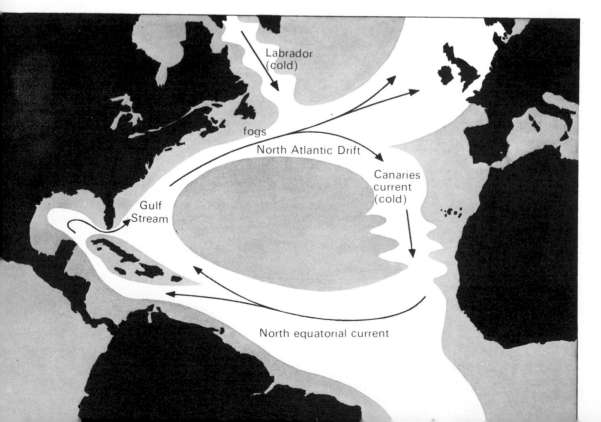

Labrador (cold)

fogs

North Atlantic Drift

Canaries current (cold)

Gulf Stream

North equatorial current

The main winds of the world all blow from high pressure regions to low pressure, but they do not blow straight. They are affected by the rotation of the Earth, which makes all moving bodies turn to their right in the northern hemisphere and to their left in the southern hemisphere. This affects winds and ocean currents, but also affects humans, who tend to walk in circles if they get lost in woods, deserts, or in foggy conditions.

The westerlies are the main winds of temperate latitudes at about 50°N and 50°S of the equator. They are south westerly in the northern hemisphere, and north westerly in the southern hemisphere. South westerly or north westerly means that they blow from the south west or north west, as winds are always named by the direction they are blowing from. Trade winds are north easterly in the northern hemisphere and south easterly in the southern hemisphere.

Winds affect the routes followed by sailing vessels. For example in the 16th to late 19th century, trade winds and westerlies helped the traffic of slaves from Africa to America and then the cotton trade from America to Europe.

Some routes also followed ocean currents. There is a circulation of oceanic waters which transfers great masses of heat from one latitude to another. The best example of this is the Gulf Stream which contains very warm water, about 25°C. When it crosses the North Atlantic it is known as the North Atlantic Drift and brings warm water to Iceland, Britain and Norway, and helps to keep coasts ice free. The climate of all these areas is much warmer than the latitude would suggest.

Shipping of slaves from West Africa. Ships rode the trade winds from Africa to the Americas and returned to Europe on the prevailing westerlies. ▼

Weather systems

Weather is always moving and always changing. Even at the equator where one day may be very similar to the next, there will be changes during the day. The morning may be sunny but soon lots of clouds will form and a shower of rain will fall in the afternoon. The evening will be clear.

At the South Pole the weather is always cold. Some days are much colder than others and the wind strength varies. There is continuous daylight for 4 to 5 months from October to February then a few weeks of twilight before 4 to 5 months of darkness from April to August.

Pressure changes are really differences in the weight of air and high pressure means heavy air. The weight of air causes an outward movement from the high pressure region (see diagram on page 10). This is how winds are formed. They are merely masses of air trying to move from a region with too much air to a region with too little.

One region with too little air is near the equator, where the rising air causes low pressure. There are other low pressure regions in the latitudes of Britain and France in the northern hemisphere, or Tasmania and New Zealand in the southern hemisphere.

▲ Hot air in the balloons is lighter than the air around it and so it rises.

A synoptic map showing weather symbols ▼

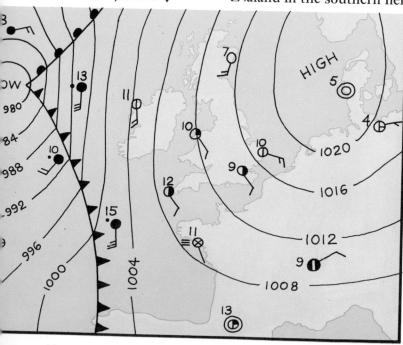

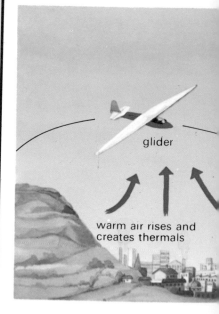

glider

warm air rises and creates thermals

Rising air will always cool and expand to form cloud and possibly rain. Falling air on the other hand is compressed and becomes warmer, just like the air in a bicycle pump when the tyre is being pumped up. Falling air creates high pressure and no rain will be formed. This is because the air is becoming warmer and warm air can hold more moisture.

If a large amount of air is moving from one place to another, it will be called an air mass, not simply a wind. Air masses will bring hot or cold, wet or dry weather, depending on where they have come from. For example an easterly air mass coming from eastern Europe to Britain in winter will bring very cold weather, because eastern Europe will be very cold at that time. Northerly winds in the USA during winter will bring very cold weather, but southerly winds will bring cold weather in Australia because the USA is in the northern hemisphere whereas Australia is in the southern.

Weather systems are shown on weather maps by a series of lines which join places of equal pressure. These are called isobars, from the Greek word 'iso' meaning the same and 'bar', a word for pressure. The isobars are numbered to indicate how high, or low the pressure is at that place (see the *synoptic map* on page 12; there are more weather symbols on page 45).

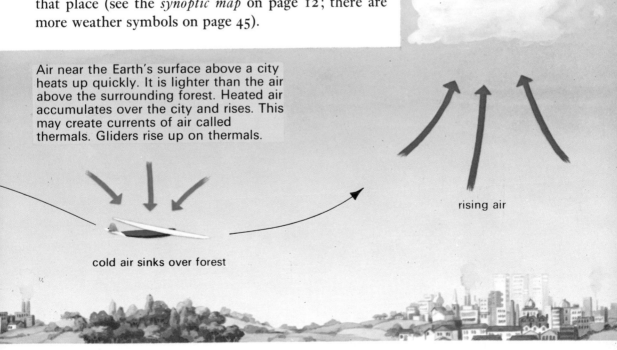

Air near the Earth's surface above a city heats up quickly. It is lighter than the air above the surrounding forest. Heated air accumulates over the city and rises. This may create currents of air called thermals. Gliders rise up on thermals.

cold air sinks over forest

rising air

Depression

Gloomy, cloudy and rainy days are generally caused by depressions which are well named, as they can be rather depressing. They are also called cyclones. They occur where two different air masses meet but do not immediately mix. This happens in some equatorial regions and in temperate latitudes too.

In the North Atlantic, cold air from the Arctic and warm air from the tropics pass alongside each other and create a whirling mass of air. This mass begins to rise and draws in more air from the sides to increase the amount of circulation and uplift. It is rather similar to water being drawn into a whirlpool.

This mass of circulating and rising air is a depression. Within the depression there will be boundary lines between the warm tropical air and the cold polar air for many days, until all the air has mixed. The dividing lines between these different masses of air are called *fronts*. The winds blow into the centre of the depression. They

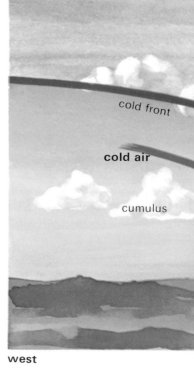

west

▲▲▲ —— cold front

◗◗◗ —— warm front

The sky after a cold front has cleared ▼

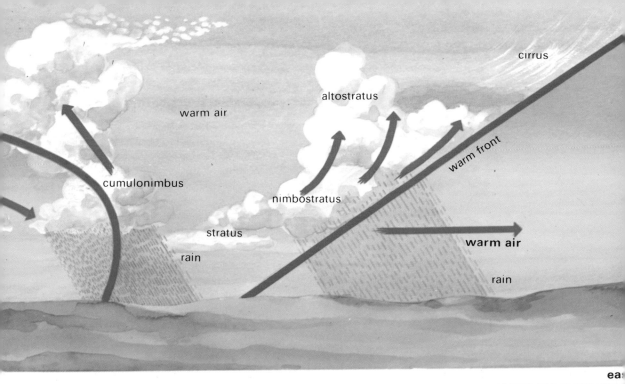

warm air

cirrus

altostratus

warm front

cumulonimbus

nimbostratus

stratus

warm air

rain

rain

ea

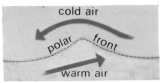

cold air

polar front

warm air

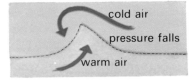

cold air

pressure falls

warm air

cold air

cold front

warm front

warm air

▲ 1. Cold air from the North Pole moves westward along the polar front. Warm air from the tropics moves eastwards.
2. A wave develops in the front as the two air masses do not mix easily. The warm air rises up over the cold air and forms a bigger bulge. The cold air curls round the back of the warm air mass.
3. Two fronts are then formed: a warm front and a cold front. The two air masses have been drawn into a circling and rising air mass. This is called a depression. The warm front will give rain, followed by a dull cloudy period. The cold front will give heavy rain.

turn to their right (in the northern hemisphere) as they travel. At the beginning of a depression in Europe or North America, the wind will be south easterly. Then it will become westerly and finally it will be northerly. The whole depression will probably be moving from west to east which is why Britain is said to have prevailing westerly winds. In reality it is prevailing westerly weather, and the winds may blow from different directions.

The depression will be shown on a weather map by a roughly circular mass of isobars which will range from about 980 or less millibars in the middle and well over 1000 on the edges. Millibars are the international units for measuring pressure, and the average atmospheric pressure in temperate latitudes is 1013.

Depressions pass over at 30–60 km/h and give rapid changes in the weather. They can bring heavy rain and yet be followed by sunshine within a few hours.

Hurricanes

Hurricanes occur in the Caribbean and other parts of the world. They are known as typhoons in eastern Asia, tropical cyclones in Bangladesh and willy-willies in Queensland, Australia.

They are like ordinary cyclones, squashed up into a smaller area, and so all their energy is more concentrated and is consequently more powerful. The source of the energy is heat from the tropical sunshine and warm tropical water.

Hurricanes all start in the tropics and travel towards the west with the prevailing movement of air of the trade winds. As they travel westwards they begin to turn to their right in the northern hemisphere or to their left in the southern hemisphere.

Hurricanes affect the West Indies and southern USA where as many as 8 can occur in an average year, mostly in the autumn. In the Indian and Pacific oceans there are usually more than twenty hurricanes a year.

They are all given names, the first of the season being called something beginning with A, the second a name beginning with B, and so on. The names always used to be girls' names, but complaints about sex discrimination in Australia and USA have led to male names being used as well.

Wherever they occur they cause vast damage. They destroy crops especially sugar cane and bananas. They can demolish houses, and they cause large waves on the sea which often flood coastlines.

In southern USA there is now an early warning system which tells people if hurricanes are likely. People can then go into underground shelters beneath their houses. The American Weather Bureau watches the hurricanes very closely, and some weather planes have actually flown into hurricanes to try to study them.

The Caribbean hurricanes have strong northerly winds of 100 knots (wind speed) or more for a few hours, followed by strong southerly winds. In the middle of

Weather service aeroplanes, such as this *Hercules*, carry instruments which record weather data at various heights. ▼

the hurricane is a calm patch known as the eye. In the eye of the storm, everything is peaceful. But then the strong winds start to blow from the other direction and the storm begins to rage again.

Much smaller than hurricanes are tornadoes which have all their energy compressed into a hundred metres or less. They may have winds of 200 knots and a funnel in the middle which sucks up dust to cause a blackened line extending from the ground to the clouds above. There are stories of animals and some humans being lifted up by the updraught. Tornadoes are most numerous in central USA. They occur most frequently in the spring but occasionally in summer or autumn. If they travel over lakes or the sea, they become water spouts. These spouts could upset small yachts or rowing boats but would not affect large boats.

▲ The eye of the storm, a photograph taken by a weather satellite in 1971. The storm was hurricane Ginger, 960 km east of Bermuda.

A tornado sweeping over Cincinnati in the United States in 1974. ▼

Anticyclones

Anticyclones are high pressure systems. They cover much greater areas than the low pressure systems. They are also much slower in their movements and may remain stationary for several days.

Anticyclones are regions of high pressure which means that the air is falling over very large areas, and therefore rain will not be formed. The winds are normally light and sunny weather is likely in summer. Calm, sunny, anticyclonic days are often followed by clear nights, during which mist or dew may form. A nice summer day in many countries often starts with dew and some mist. The sun gradually evaporates the moisture to give a lovely hot day.

These are the days when it is pleasant to go to the beach, but winds often develop at the seaside during anticyclones. During the day, the land becomes much hotter than the sea and, on a small or local scale, the air starts to rise.

This rising air is replaced by wind drifting in from the sea during the afternoons. This is a sea breeze. At night, the land is cooler than the sea and so a wind blows out from land to sea. This is the land breeze.

These land and sea breezes explain why it is often cooler on the beach on a lovely sunny day than it is inland. On the coast the sea breeze feels quite cold. Many primitive fishermen have used land and sea breezes for centuries. They sail out with the land breeze early in the morning, and are blown back to land with the sea breeze early in the afternoon.

There are sometimes bulges in anticyclones which are called ridges. Ridges extending from the Azores high pressure region and the Saharan high will sometimes bring sunshine to Britain in summer.

Not all anticyclones give hot sunny weather. There are anticyclones permanently located near the North and South Poles where the cold air creates high pressure systems. Ridges extending southwards from the Arctic high pressure will often bring cold weather to parts of Europe and North America in winter.

▲ Fishermen often use offshore winds to go out to sea in the morning, and then onshore winds blow them back early in the afternoon. Here are some fishermen from Bali, Indonesia, returning home. The afternoon winds will often make the beach quite cool, and may discourage sunbathing even on a nice sunny day.

A sea breeze. ▶

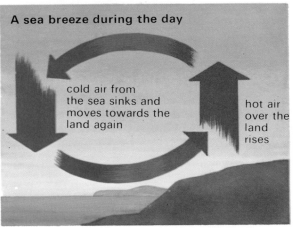

A sea breeze during the day

cold air from the sea sinks and moves towards the land again

hot air over the land rises

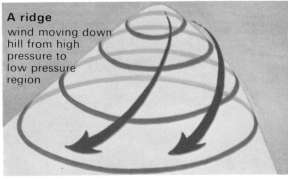

A ridge
wind moving down hill from high pressure to low pressure region

Winds blow out from the high pressure turning to their right in the northern hemisphere.

Anticyclonic conditions

There are many high pressure systems which cover large areas around the Tropics of Capricorn and Cancer. These anticyclones are found in the Horse Latitudes and they cause hot and dry conditions.

Permanent high pressure near North Africa has produced the Sahara desert where it is hot and sunny every day. *Shade temperatures* during the day reach 40°C and in the sun, rocks become so hot that eggs can be fried on them. At night the temperature falls, sometimes to freezing point. The maximum recorded range of temperature in a 24 hour period is over 55°C.

Rain is rare in deserts, but occasional thunderstorms occur. They bring very heavy rain which may only last a few minutes. These downpours may create rivers which flow like torrents for a few hours and then slow down and disappear.

There are no permanent rivers in the Sahara, except for the Nile, which is supplied by water from Kenya and Ethiopia where rainfall is heavier. The Nile has few tributaries bringing in extra water, and because of evaporation, it becomes smaller and smaller as it travels across the desert.

The high pressure which influences the Sahara throughout the year also affects other areas. In June, July and August, the Mediterranean lands have the Horse Latitudes high pressure system which is at its most northerly point. The Azores high is part of this high pressure system and one source of the anticyclones which occasionally bring sunny summer weather to Britain.

The Mediterranean summers have temperatures of about 25°C. The plants shrivel in the heat, and the vegetation has to adapt to survive the summer drought. Some trees have thick bark, such as on the cork oak. Others, such as the olive, have long roots to reach underground water. Others have waxy leaves or spines which do not lose moisture.

People have a 'siesta' (or afternoon sleep) during the hottest time of the day. They have light-coloured houses

▲ The dry lands of Niger are affected by high pressure system.

July winds shown blowing away from high pressure areas. ▶

◀ Animals, such as these waterbucks in Southern Africa, have to migrate during the dry season.

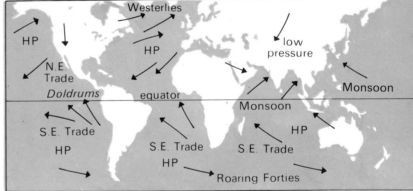

because white reflects the heat. The windows are small and shuttered to keep the interiors cool.

The high pressure system moves south, away from the Mediterranean in the autumn. It still affects the Sahara, but also covers the savanna lands in the north of Nigeria, Sudan and elsewhere.

In the savanna lands the grass which grows up to two metres in the hot wet summer shrivels up in the hot dry winter. As in the desert, trees survive by having long roots, thorns or the ability to store water inside the trunk, as in the case of the bottle tree and baobab. Animals have to travel during the dry season, in the search for food, and water holes become vital to all forms of life.

Clouds

Cirrus clouds (above 6,000 m)

Clouds are made of masses of tiny drops of water. Each drop is only 0.01 mm in diameter, and every drop forms on or round a solid object such as a particle of dust. The drops collide with others and become larger, until they can be seen and eventually may become heavy enough to fall as rain.

Clouds form by air cooling, either as a result of air rising or because of one mass of air mixing with another, cooler, air mass. The water vapour in the air condenses into a visible droplet. This is rather similar to hot air coming out of a hot kettle which condenses to form steam as soon as it mixes with cooler air outside the kettle.

There are three main different types of cloud but many variations of these three

◄ Altocumulus (between 3,000 and 6,000 m)

Cumulonimbus (below 2,000 m) ▼

occur. Clouds with a flat base with a dome on top are called cumulus. These look like white fluffy cauliflowers or pieces of cotton wool, all heaped up. They are the result of an uprush of air which has caused condensation. If the uprush is very rapid, large and numerous drops of water may condense and a darker cloud will then form. This cloud will be called cumulonimbus.

A nice fluffy white cumulus will not give any rain but the darker the cloud becomes, the greater the likelihood of rain. Cumulonimbus clouds consist of ice crystals high up in the sky. They are dark thunder clouds which bring heavy rain and lightning.

Clouds which extend outwards in sheets are called stratus. They may be light grey in colour, very thin and unlikely to give rain on their own. But thicker and darker stratus may give some steady and light rain.

Stratus and cumulus both consist of water droplets but the third type, cirrus, is made up of ice crystals. Cirrus are the highest clouds and are very thin and wispy. As they are accumulations of ice crystals, they let the sun shine through them.

There are all sorts of combinations such as stratocumulus. There are alto-stratus or altocumulus, and even cirro-stratus. Clouds occasionally may be a help with forecasting. For example if a large mass of cloud is seen approaching it may foretell a depression. Altostratus are a sign of bad weather.

Clouds are affected by high mountains, such as the Matterhorn for instance, and many ranges are covered by clouds for half the days in the year.

Cloud over the Matterhorn mountain. As air over the mountain cools, it releases its water vapour and forms a cloud.

Winds and rain

Prevailing winds on a large or world scale are called planetary winds. These are the trades, westerlies and polar winds. There are also local winds which affect smaller areas. For example there are the land and sea breezes, or the Mistral which blows down the Rhône valley, or the Chinook which blows from the Rockies onto the Canadian Prairies.

Wind has an important effect on life. In some cases the absence of wind may mean there is fog or a thunderstorm coming, but too much wind may uproot trees. Winds may affect high lorries on exposed roads, but they are very important to yachtsmen. One standard method for measuring wind is by means of the Beaufort scale (see table above).

There are strong movements in the upper air levels which may affect aircraft. These are high speed winds called jet streams. If a jet stream follows the aircraft it may increase its speed. If the aircraft runs into a jet stream it may be slowed down.

The windiest place in the world is said to be on the edge of Antarctica where the average speed is over 60 km/h. Wind speeds of over 100 km/h occur on one day in three. Highest recorded gusts of wind are over 370 km/h on Mt. Washington in the USA.

All winds are the result of the pressure gradient and merely represent air going from high pressure to somewhere with lower pressure. The pressure gradient is the movement of air downwards similar to a cyclist freewheeling downhill. The steeper the hill the faster the cyclist will

travel. The steeper the pressure gradient the faster the wind will blow. If isobars on the weather map are very close together, the gradient is very steep.

Rain and thunder

Rain is caused by air rising and then cooling, as in the formation of cloud. The air rises until the cooling forms drops which are heavy enough to fall. The maximum size reached is about 2.5 mm in diameter.

There are three types of rainfall, frontal or cyclonic, convective and relief. Frontal rainfall is associated with fronts in a depression and falls because of the air which is rising along the fronts.

Convection rainfall is caused by heat. The hot air rises and then expands and cools. As it cools condensation takes place and rain drops form. Thunder and

Beaufort scale	Effect	Speed (km/h)
0 Calm		
1 Light air	Drift of smoke	1–5
2 Light breeze	Leaves rustle	6–11
3 Gentle breeze	Leaves and twigs in constant motion	12–19
4 Moderate breeze	Dust raised, small branches move	20–29
5 Fresh breeze	Small trees begin to sway	30–36
6 Strong breeze	Large branches move, telephone wires whistle	37–49
7 Near gale	Whole trees move	50–60
8 Gale	Twigs break off trees, walking is difficult	61–73
9 Severe gale	Slight damage to houses	74–86
10 Storm	Trees uprooted, much damage to houses	87–100
11 Violent storm	Widespread damage	101–120
12 Hurricane	Excessive damage	above 121

Lightning strikes the Empire State Building in New York, USA. ▶

lightning occur in convection storms. The electric charges which give lightning also cause the noise of thunder. We see the lightning before we hear thunder because the light travels faster than the noise. Relief rain results from air being cooled because it has to rise to pass over mountains.

Amounts of rain may be very varied in different places. For example a weather station at Cherrapunji in India receives nearly 11,000 mm per annum, but another station in India, in the Thar desert, receives less than 250 mm. In Britain the wettest areas are the mountains in the north west where 5,000 mm may fall. In south east England the annual total may be less than 600 mm.

Snow and hail

Hail is frozen rain and consists of layers of ice caused by uprushes of air. If a drop of water is pushed up by a rising *convection current*, the higher it goes the colder it will get. The drop may go so high that it will freeze. It will eventually fall and more water will cling to it so that if it is lifted up again by the convection current a second layer of ice will form. This may happen several times, but eventually the hailstone will fall to the ground. Large stones may weigh up to 500 grams and can break windows and greenhouses, kill chickens and hurt larger animals.

The largest hailstone to be measured was 190 mm in diameter and weighed 758 grams. It fell at Coffeyville in Kansas USA in 1970. Hailstorms are particularly frequent in hot countries especially in the middle of large land masses. India is a frequent sufferer from violent hail storms.

In Britain hailstones rarely exceed pea size, but there are some records of hailstones the size of golf balls. They weigh more than 100 grams and can completely flatten crops. A dramatic hailstorm affected parts of Wiltshire in July 1967, when stones with diameters of seventy five millimetres broke thousands of panes of glass.

Snow is frozen water vapour and the ice particles solidify onto solid particles such as specks of dust. The ice crystals all have six points and many tiny crystals cling together to make a flake of snow. Every snow flake is unique because of the wide variety of ways in which the crystals can cling together.

Snow may be very wet and clingy, good for making snowballs or snowmen, if the temperature is near freezing. Some snow is quite dry and powdery, unsuitable for snowballs, and can be cleared from roads by a snow blower. Wet snow needs a snowplough. On average, ten centimetres of snow will contain as much water as about one centimetre of rain.

Many places in the Rocky Mountains, Western Norway and southern Chile receive from 5,000 to 10,000 mm of snow in a year. A weather station on Mt. Rainier in Washington USA has recorded more than 31,000 mm in

▲ Different patterns of snow flakes. They always have six sides.

Avalanches are killers. They destroy everything as they slide down mountains and finally bury villages under tons of snow. ▶

a year. In Britain over 1,500 mm is sometimes recorded in Wales and the Lake District for instance.

Snow is welcome in some places as it is important for skiing and helps to provide a good source of income in tourist areas. It is also useful for protecting the soil from frost, because a cover of snow will enable crops to survive even severe frosts. Snow is also useful in some places when it melts as it provides a source of water.

There are obviously some disadvantages attached to snowfalls however. They can often block roads. Snow can also come downhill in avalanches. These can be very destructive, as they may flatten trees and houses.

Frost, fog and dew

Dew forms as air cools, especially in calm anticyclonic conditions. Summer and autumn mornings will often start with the ground soaked with dew. As anticyclonic conditions are ideal for dew, there will normally be sunny days which will quickly evaporate the dew.

Some locations, for example the Sahara, will have dew every morning, and there are plants which can survive on moisture from dew in areas where there is no rainfall. Dew settles on all objects including stones, grass and bushes.

If dew freezes, it will form frost, which therefore is also associated with anticyclonic conditions. When the temperature falls below freezing point, frost forms first on the ground, and then, as the air above the surface is cooled, air frost will form. Anyone driving a car in these sort of conditions will need a de-icing substance to clear frost off the windscreen.

Ponds will freeze over, and each day of continuing frosty conditions will make the ice thicker. Several days of frost will be required before the ice becomes thick and strong enough for skating.

When water freezes it expands by about 9% of its volume and so it occupies more space. This is the reason for burst water pipes. If the water in a pipe becomes frozen, the water will expand and may split the pipe. When the thaw sets in and the ice melts the water will flow out through the hole created.

It is sometimes possible to see bottles of milk in which the cream has frozen. The expansion will push the milk bottle top away from the bottle and leave it

Frosted leaves ▼

perched like a cap on a column of ice. This is an experiment which can be tried in frosty weather.

If a sponge is put into a dish of water, it will start to soak up the water. Eventually it will become saturated and then will not be able to pick up any more water. Air is like this and when it becomes saturated it forms mist or fog.

These result from the presence of water particles floating in the air. If it is not possible to see further ahead than 1,000 metres it is called fog, but otherwise it is called mist. Fog and mist normally form in the evenings when the ground is cooling. The cold ground cools the air above by contact.

The cool air is heavier than the warmer air, and so it begins to roll downhill and will normally build up in valleys. Valleys are also likely locations for fog to accumulate because the rivers will provide extra moisture.

In the autumn, after a nice sunny day, it is often possible to see a layer of mist just above the ground, but only a metre or so in height. Mist which occurs on mountain sides is different, as this is really low-level cloud.

Fog and frost can cause travel problems. In icy conditions great care is required on the roads, and aircraft have to avoid icing problems. Foggy conditions often cause accidents on the roads.

Aircraft can use radar, and at some airports can land 'blind', when visibility is virtually nil. The pilots have to rely entirely on information provided by instruments.

Dew on spider's web ▼

Effects of altitude

Temperatures decrease the higher one gets above sea level. In spite of this it may feel very hot for walkers who are going uphill, and skiers in mountain resorts will often become very sunburnt.

The average rate of temperature decrease is 1°C for every 160 metres. This is why there may be snow lying on a high mountain top when green vegetation may be seen down in the valley.

The sun's rays heat the surface of the Earth. In turn, the ground heats the air above, so the warmest air is closest to the ground. The reason for the loss of temperature is the thickness or density of the atmosphere. The denser the air, the more water vapour and dust particles there will be to absorb warmth. In high mountains the atmosphere is much thinner and so even though the same amount of heat may be brought by rays of sunlight, not so much can be absorbed.

The changes in climate affect vegetation, which also changes with height. In the Alps there are often cultivated areas and deciduous forests in the lower places, but from about 1,400 to 1,900 metres there is normally coniferous forest. Deciduous trees shed their leaves during the autumn in order to survive whereas coniferous trees have hard needles which hold moisture. This helps to keep them alive too. Higher up, the trees thin out as the temperature becomes lower, and grassland is the main vegetation. Above the grassland zone there is barren ground and higher still there will be snow and ice.

Atmospheric pressure decreases steadily with altitude. At sea level the average pressure is about 1013 millibars, but at 1,000 metres has fallen to less than 900 millibars. At 2,000 metres the pressure is less than 800 millibars.

The change in pressure can affect people. Anyone who lives high in mountains such as Bolivia will have larger lungs than people living near sea level. This enables them to breathe successfully in the rarefied or thinner air. Athletes from high areas seem to have larger lungs and can run well at low altitudes.

coniferous forest

deciduous forest

temperate pasture

▲ Lush vegetation is found in hot wet lowlands, and trees will grow on mountain sides wherever there is sufficient rainfall. When temperatures fall and the air becomes cooler, deciduous trees cannot survive and so coniferous forests are found. Above the trees, there will be a belt of grassland and finally bare rock and snow.

The Cordillera Real mountain in Bolivia is just under 6,000 m high. Bolivian people are used to the altitude. ▶

snow and ice

sparse vegetation

lowland forest

▲ Athletes suffering from lack of oxygen at the Mexico Olympics in 1968. People used to air pressure at sea level find it difficult to breathe at high altitude.

Local climate

Small areas can have their own climates and the study of the local weather of small areas is called micro-climatology. For example, plants may find shelter behind a wall or a hedge, and people may find shelter behind a windbreak or a·break-water on a beach.

There are differences between towns and the surrounding countryside. Towns, or urban areas are warmer than rural areas because all the buildings soak up heat and retain it. There is also heat being given off by central heating and by people. Districts which contain closely-packed houses will be a degree or two warmer than more widely spaced houses with large gardens. Towns often have a dusty or even polluted atmosphere which prevents the sun's rays from getting through. There is more sunshine in rural areas than in the towns.

London used to be particularly notorious for its lack of sunshine, which was often less than half the amount received in the surrounding countryside. The Clean Air Act of 1956 made it an offence to pollute the air. Since then, London has become cleaner and sunnier.

There is yet another difference between cities and the countryside: cities are less windy, because of the friction created by the buildings. They stop or reduce the flow of wind, although in some places they cause funnelling which gives very strong winds on a few street corners.

Many isolated houses on the Prairies or Pampas are surrounded by trees. These have been planted to provide shelter from the wind. They create their own micro-climate.

There are often differences between hills and valleys, even if these features are quite small. Hills are more exposed and will be windier, never as hot as

Gardens have their own micro-climates. Some plants grow behind walls protected from the wind, others grow between rocks and get warmth from the sun baking the paving stones. ▼

valleys in summer, but never as cold in winter. Valleys can become scorching hot, but at night, cold air may roll down the slopes and accumulate in the hollow.

Mist will form and eventually there will be frost. Hollows in British valleys often have slight frosts when the higher ground stays just above freezing point. Some large valleys in Switzerland have regular night frosts which kill off and blacken the vegetation. Above the blackened level there may be vines and fruit trees growing.

Los Angeles is in a hollow and here the fog often accumulates, and is made worse by pollution from car exhaust systems. This fog plus smoke, is called smog and it can damage lungs. Many towns noted for grime and smog have been cleaned up like Sheffield in England.

▲ Mist in hollow of the Dyffryn valley in Snowdonia, Wales.

Wind blowing round a street corner. ▼

Weather instruments

Temperatures are measured by thermometers. Ordinary thermometers can be used to read off the temperature at any given time.

Maximum-minimum thermometers contain metal rods which are pushed along the tube by the mercury or alcohol they contain. These rods are left behind at the highest and lowest temperatures reached by the thermometer. Normally the maximum and minimum temperatures will be read at about 8 or 9 o'clock in the morning. The rods can be moved back ready to start another day, by the use of a magnet which will pull the rods along the tube.

The lowest temperature near the ground is recorded by a grass minimum thermometer. This also has a metal rod to mark the lowest point reached during the night.

Pressure is recorded by a barometer, the best type being a mercury barometer which is large and expensive. An aneroid is much smaller and cheaper, and is the type used in domestic barometers.

Barographs also use aneroids. A barograph consists of a piece of paper on a revolving drum. A clock inside this drum turns it round very slowly, one complete turn every week. A pen moves up and down with pressure changes. The nib on this pen rests on the rotating piece of paper and writes a continuous record of pressure changes throughout the week.

Wind is recorded by an anemometer. There are many different kinds. Some merely show the wind speed on a dial, which has to be looked at by an observer. Others keep a record of wind speed and also wind direction. Rain gauges and sunshine recorders are also useful.

A Stevenson screen is an essential part of a weather station. It is a light-coloured box on legs which contains many of the essential weather instruments.

It is possible for a keen amateur to keep some interesting records with cheaper instruments. A Six's thermometer will record maximum and minimum temperatures, and rain gauges and Stevenson screens can be home made.

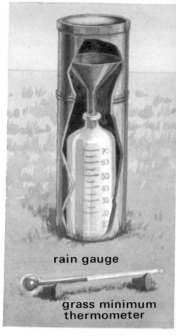

rain gauge

grass minimum thermometer

Taking records from a Stevenson screen. In the weather station the following instruments are kept: a rain gauge, a grass minimum thermometer, a Stevenson screen, soil thermometers, an anemometer, a barometer and a sunshine recorder. ▶

aneroid barometer

▲ A barometer will contain an aneroid, which expands or contracts as pressure changes.

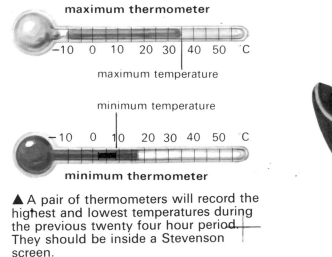

maximum thermometer

-10　0　10　20　30　40　50　°C

maximum temperature

minimum temperature

-10　0　10　20　30　40　50　°C

minimum thermometer

▲ A pair of thermometers will record the highest and lowest temperatures during the previous twenty four hour period. They should be inside a Stevenson screen.

sunshine recorder

Collecting information

In Britain there are more than 300 weather stations which collect information and send it to Bracknell in Berkshire where the British Meteorological Office is located. There are also weather ships in the North Atlantic which supply information. Masses of data are also sent from the weather centre in Frankfurt, West Germany. More information on weather is received from weather aircraft, weather balloons called radio sondes and ship to shore stations. They send weather reports to land stations by radio.

Washington in the USA and Frankfurt are the great collecting centres for weather information from all over the world. There has been world cooperation in weather information for many years, and teleprinters send information from one country to another. There is now information provided by space satellites. They take photographs of weather systems in the troposphere.

The information is sorted out and maps are drawn to show the present situation. A forecast can then be made. Meanwhile the next map is being drawn using later information, and this is a permanent occupation as the weather keeps changing, and new maps are required.

Forecasting is based on knowledge and there is never enough information available to be absolutely sure about what the weather is going to do next.

More knowledge means better forecasting, and experts are more likely to give good forecasts than less knowledgeable amateurs.

Weather forecasts for the next few hours are normally very good, but if made for two or three days ahead they are less likely to be accurate. The Meteorological Office now issues long range forecasts for the next month. These are only general forecasts about the likely types of weather, and do not give precise details. They are based on studies made of past weather conditions.

It is always interesting to try to make your own forecasts. Look at the pressure changes on your barometer. If the pressure is rising more settled weather is likely, but if it is falling, wind and rain become more likely.

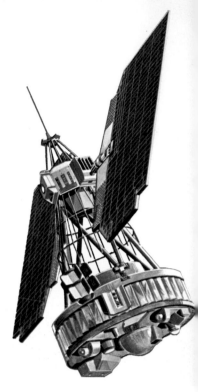

▲ The Nimbus weather satellite takes photographs of the Earth. Its wings face the sun and help produce energy to make instruments work. The base of the satellite always faces the Earth. The cameras are placed in the base.

A less scientific way of forecasting weather! ▶

▲ Michael Fish, a television weather forecaster.

A satellite photograph showing the UK covered with cumulus clouds. ▼

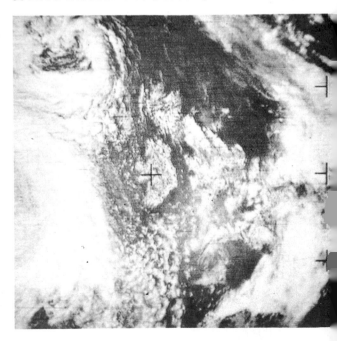

Regional variations

The Mediterranean lands have hot sunny summers because of the influence of the Saharan high pressure system, and temperatures reach 25°C daily. The heat and sunshine are good for ripening wheat and barley, and fruits such as oranges, olives and grapes. The sunshine helps to produce dried fruits, prunes, currants and raisins. There is a shortage of water for crop growing in summer, but irrigation helps to overcome this problem. The sunshine attracts many tourists from Britain, Germany and Scandinavia.

Further east in Europe are the steppes, where summers are quite hot, more than 20°C, and there is convection rain. Winters are very cold, ten or twenty degrees below freezing, and a continental high pressure system builds up.

The people above, huddled up on a British beach may well wish they were taking their holiday in a warmer place such as Albufeira, Portugal, below.

Further east and north in Siberia, winter temperatures fall as low as forty or fifty degrees below freezing at Verkhoyansk. People have to remain indoors as much as possible, houses have to be well insulated, and double or even treble glazing is necessary. The former primitive inhabitants used to build stone and earth houses which were completely air tight, and the thick walls meant that there was no loss of heat from the inside.

On the coast of northern Europe in Norway, winters are mild and wet. Conditions are good for trees, and wood is used for most of the houses. Low pressure prevails for most of the year, and mild damp conditions are common. Inland there are high mountains and there is much snow. This has helped to encourage a tourist industry, and the mountains have waterfalls which are useful for generating hydro-electricity.

Britain has mild, wet winters, similar to those of south west Norway, but there is better weather in summer because the Azores high pressure system brings some sunny weather. However, hot weather is still not guaranteed, which is why many people go to other countries for their holidays.

Other continents also show variations in weather conditions. In North America there are parts of California which are quite similar to the Mediterranean. British Columbia and Washington State are similar to Britain, and Alaska has areas which resemble Norway. The Prairies resemble the Steppes in weather conditions, and northern Canada is similar to northern Finland and Russia. Europe has no east coast and so eastern North America has no comparable areas in Europe, but there are similarities with parts of Asia.

In the Arctic, the weather is always cold and so people need to wear warm, fur-lined clothes.

Changing climate

In temperate latitudes, there are daily weather changes, and one month is different from the next. Also each year is slightly different from all others, but there are no great changes in a ten or fifty year period. An occasional summer which is hotter than average, or a winter colder than average does not signify a real climatic change.

Since the Ice Age, the climate of Britain has warmed up, but there have been many fluctuations. For example there were cold years in the Middle Ages and the Thames froze up. Fairs were held on the ice in many winters. People started putting windows in their houses at about this time to keep the cold out.

Changes since the Ice Age have been slow and slight, but the Ice Age itself represents an enormous difference. Most of England, and the whole of Scotland and Wales were covered by an ice sheet.

▲ In the late 17th century, winters in Europe were colder than today. The Thames often froze as this print shows and people used to go skating on the river.

All forms of life migrated southwards though in the warmer phases when the ice melted for a few centuries, humans and animals such as mammoths moved northwards over Britain. Tundra conditions which exist in Canada and northern Asia today prevailed in southern England whilst the ice covered the north and arctic animals roamed the land. At this time, the Sahara was probably much smaller as all the climatic belts would be compressed. There would have been more rain in the northern Sahara and permanent rivers carved the valleys which are now usually empty.

Rocks tell of older climatic changes than the Ice Age. Salt deposits indicate former desert conditions often millions of years ago. There may also be deposits of some very smooth rounded grains of

▲ The annual rings of trees, such as this Bristle cone pine, record years of climate change.

sand called millet seed sands which have been formed by wind blowing them along the ground. They are smoothed as they travel, and they are evidence of desert climatic conditions in the past.

Hills in northern England and many other temperate locations contain coral fossils, and the coral animal could have only lived in warm tropical seas. There are coal deposits in Pennsylvania, Manchuria and many other locations, and these are the relics of sub-tropical deltas.

The warm-up since the last ice advance has had important effects on sea level as warmer weather melts ice. The Bering Straits and the Straits of Dover have formed where dry land used to be because the sea level has risen in the last few thousand years. The sea has risen about 100 metres in the last 10,000 years, and there is enough ice left to make the sea rise another 100 metres, if it all melted. If the sea did rise by so much, many large cities such as London and New York would be flooded.

The growth rings on trees will also reveal information about which years were wet and good for tree growth.

▲ In 1883 the Krakatoa volcano situated between Java and Sumatra exploded and 30,000 people were killed. The volcano threw up dust which remained in the atmosphere for three years. This produced climatic changes. It also caused sunsets in many places.

Weather and people

Weather and climate affect the ways of life of people everywhere. It affects people's working lives as well as their leisure time. A sudden cold spell is as disastrous for the farmer as for the fisherman. It may ruin crops by bringing frost and it makes trawling for fish very unpleasant when the ice covers the trawlers. Weather also limits what the farmer can grow, for example, some places can grow rice, whereas others will grow wheat. Apples will grow in some countries and bananas will grow in others.

Trade makes it possible to obtain foods from different climates, and the use of glasshouses helps to grow them despite the climate. Bananas are grown in Reykjavik in Iceland using warm water from the geysers. Irrigation in deserts is another way in which people can overcome the restrictions caused by the climate.

Habits may be caused or influenced by the weather. Some people wear shorts, or possibly nothing at all, and can eat their meals out of doors. In Britain it is normally too cold to eat outside, and even in summer, plans for picnics may be ruined by a rapid change in the weather.

Rain may not always be popular, but some places do not have enough. In parts of USA, Australia and South Africa attempts have been made to 'seed' clouds to make them drop some rain. Planes fly into the clouds and drop silver iodide or salt crystals in the hope that water particles will condense on them and help to create rain. Some rain may fall, but other places further on may then get less rain.

◀ Villagers digging for water in Ethiopia in 1973. Droughts suddenly hit southern Africa in the 1970s and people as well as livestock suffered as a result.

▲ Forest being cleared in Papua, New Guinea. The removal of too many trees can upset the balance of nature and it may eventually change the contents of the atmosphere.

Thousands of trees have been planted in the Sahara to make more rain fall. Although they needed daily watering at first, they can now survive without extra water, possibly because they make the atmosphere damper.

In another part of the world, removal of trees may be causing changes. Much of the Amazon forest is being removed, for road-making schemes or farming developments in Brazil. If all the trees are removed there might be too much carbon dioxide in the air which could affect animals. Trees normally consume carbon dioxide and give off oxygen, whereas animals use oxygen and give off carbon dioxide and a nice state of balance has been achieved in the past. The influence of people adds to the complexities and ever-changing patterns of weather.

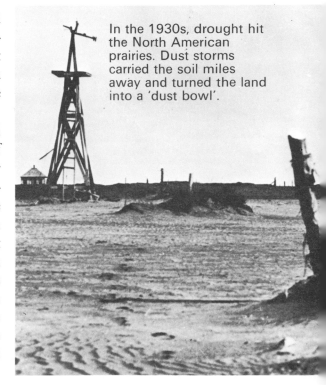

In the 1930s, drought hit the North American prairies. Dust storms carried the soil miles away and turned the land into a 'dust bowl'.

Books to read

Weather, George Bosnall; Grosset and Dunlap
The Weather, F. Dalton; Crane, Russak & Co. 1978
Your Environment: Air, Air Pollution and Weather, Collins M. Henson; Interstate 1971
Winds and Weather, John Kaufmann; William Morrow 1971
Weather and Climate, Seymour Simon; Random House 1969
Way of the Weather, Jerome Spar; Creative Education 1967
Everyday Weather and How It Works, Herman Schneider; McGraw-Hill 1961
Understanding Weather, H. Milgrom; Macmillan 1970

Things to do

Local museums and large science museums often have old weather instruments which you can look at. Visit a weather center which may be found in large cities and sometimes in holiday resorts. Meteorological stations can often be seen at airports or at universities.

Keep a weather diary. Take your own records if you have any weather instruments. If you have not, look in the daily papers where temperatures for the previous 24 hours will be given.

Use the temperatures for several weather stations in the United States and Canada to see how the temperature will vary in different places on one day. Read the weather forecast, or watch it on television and then notice the weather to see if the forecast is correct. If it goes wrong try and find out why. It is normally the result of a weather system such as a depression travelling a little faster than expected, or because it has changed direction slightly. If this happens, a belt of rain may pass further north (or south) than expected. As a result some people will then receive rain which was not expected, whilst other people who were forecast rain may in fact have a dry day.

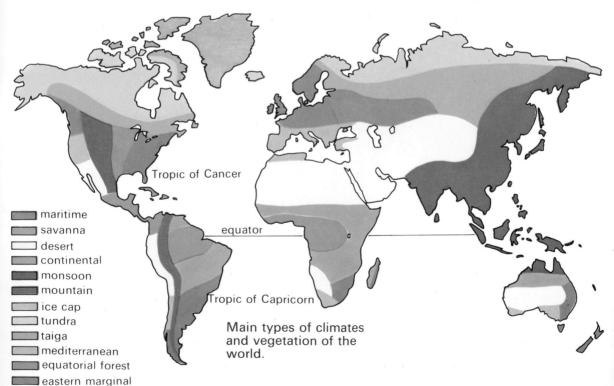

Tropic of Cancer

equator

Tropic of Capricorn

- maritime
- savanna
- desert
- continental
- monsoon
- mountain
- ice cap
- tundra
- taiga
- mediterranean
- equatorial forest
- eastern marginal

Main types of climates and vegetation of the world.

WEATHER SYMBOLS

⦁	drizzle
▽	shower
●	rain
✳	snow
△	hail
⏦	thunderstorm
⦁✳	sleet
⦂●	heavy rain
✳▽	snow shower
⌒⌒⌒	warm front
▲▲▲	cold front
═	mist
☰	fog

WIND SYMBOLS

◎	calm
	1-2 knots
	3-7 knots
	8-12 knots
	13-17 knots

Additional half feathers are each worth 5 knots

	50 knots or more

Cloud cover in eighths of the sky

◔	clear	◓	5
◑	1	◕	6
◔	2	◕	7
◕	3	●	8
◑	4	⊗	obscured

Glossary

Here is a list of some of the more difficult terms used in this book.

Convection currents: Heat causes air to rise in what is called a convection current. If water is heated it will start to move and that is also called convection.

Drizzle: Light rain which consists of drops of water not large enough to be called raindrops, but too large to be floating without falling.

Drought: A shortage of water.

Föhn: This is a local wind which affects Alpine valleys. It is a warm wind similar to the Chinook.

Hoar frost: Frost that deposits rime.

Humidity: This is the amount of water vapour in the air. If the humidity is high, mist or rain may occur.

Maritime: Climates affected by the sea are said to have maritime influences. Maritime climates are wet and usually much warmer in winter.

Monsoon: The word means seasonal and refers to the seasonal change of wind direction. Monsoon areas such as India or China have winds blowing from the sea to the land throughout the summer, and these are wet winds. In winter the winds are dry as they blow from land to sea.

Occlusion: An occlusion, or occluded front, is a combination of a warm and cold front. A cold front will often catch up with a warm front to form an occlusion.

Shade temperatures: Official temperature records are always taken in the shade, preferably inside a Stevenson screen.

Sleet: This is half way between rain and snow. It is usually snow which melts on its way down to the ground because the temperature is just above zero.

Synoptic chart: Weather map produced by the Meteorological Office. It is a chart or map which gives a synopsis or summary of the weather situation.

Thermograph: Instrument which is like a barograph as it gives a continuous record for a week, but it records temperature and not pressure.

Trade winds: Tropical winds which blow towards the equator.

Trough: Extension or bulge from a depression. It is part of a low pressure system and will probably contain a front.

Westerlies: These are the temperate winds which blow away from the tropics towards the temperate latitudes.

Index

Illustrations appear in bold
type